HISTORY OF THE COLLIE

The early history of the Collie is vague because, apparently, the dog was so common that few contemporary writers remarked upon it. One who did was Dr. John Caius writing in 1570. He has this to say about the shepherd's dog we now call the Collie:

Our shepherd's dog is not huge, and vast, and big, but of an indifferent stature and growth, because it has not to deal with the bloodthirsty wolf, since there be none in England...This dog, either at the hearing of his master's voice, or at the wagging of his fist, or at his shrill and hoarse whistling and hissing, bringeth the wandering wethers and stray sheep into the self—same place where the master's will and work is to have them, whereby the shepherd reapeth the benefit, namely, that with a little labour and no toil of moving his feet, he may rule and guide his flock according to his own desire, either to have them go forward or stand still, or to draw backward, or to turn this way, or take that way. For it is not in England as it is in France, as it is in Flanders, as it is in Syria, as it is in Tartary, where the sheep follow the shepherd, for here in our country the shepherd followeth the sheep, and sometimes the straying sheep, when no dog runs before them, nor goeth about and beside them, gather themselves into a flock, when they hear the shepherd whistle, for fear of the dog (as I imagine), remembering that (if unreasoning creatures may be reported to have memory) the dog commonly runneth out as his master's warrant, which is his whistle. This have we oftentimes marked when we have taken our journey from town to town; when we have heard a shepherd whistle, we have reined in our horse and stood still a space to see the proof and trial of this matter. Furthermore with the dog doth the shepherd take the sheep to slaughter, and to be healed if they be sick, and no hurt or harm is done by the dogs to the simple creature.

Collies have been used as shepherd and companion dogs for more than 400 years.

HOW COLLIE GOT HIS NAME

The origin of the name "Collie" is somewhat in doubt. Some say it came from Coaly, referring to the color of the dogs, as black was probably the predominant color in the original breed. Others claim it comes from Colley, a breed of Scottish sheep. In any event, the Collie gradually increased in size, his head became longer and more refined, his coat longer and gait more stylish, until he reached the appearance which will make any child exclaim, "Oh, look at the pretty dog!" Queen Victoria was a patroness of the breed and had a considerable amount to do with

Collies originated in Scotland and the border country of northern England. Their names were originally spelled *Colley*.

breed undoubtedly originated in Scotland and the border country of northern England, where it remained strictly a utilitarian breed until the 19th century. It was after the Collie attracted the interest of English breeders that it became popular and at the same time, more glamorous. These fanciers bred selectively, picking as parents the dogs which in looks and temperament would be popular as house pets and family dogs as well as workers. And so its rise in popularity. Since 1900, when a boom in Collies began in this country, with wealthy men such as J.P. Morgan, importing and exhibiting them, the breed ideal has changed very little. There are just more Collies, and more good ones, then there were in those days.

Rawdon B. Lee, a 19th century dog historian, has traced the derivation of the Collie's name. He tells us that it was originally spelled Colley, and that it comes from the Anglo-Saxon word for black—"col". The black-faced sheep of Scotland were once called "colleys" so, naturally, the dog that drove them came to be known as "colley dog." Shakespeare uses the word in its meaning of black in his play, *A Midsummer Night's Dream,* when he says, "Brief as the lightening in the collied night"; and Chaucer mentions "Coll our dog." Our word "coal" comes from the same source.

This derivation seems simple enough, yet there are other old writers who question it. One would have it that the Collie is so called because of the white band around his neck, suggesting a natural collar. Another claims that it comes from the Gaelic since the word in that ancient language for a whelp or puppy is cuilean.

It was once believed in Scotland that the Deerhound, the Collie, and the Scottish Terrier were all descended from a common ancestor since there was a great similarity in the shape of the head, expression and ears of

The name *collie* derived from the old Anglo-Saxon word *col* which means *black* (also think of *coal*). These dogs tended sheep which had a black face and were called *colleys*. Thus the dogs tending the *colleys* were called *colley dogs*.

these three breeds at that time. Another historian has it that the Newfoundland played a part in the Collie's early development.

Rawdon Lee tells this story of a traveller in the Cumberland Lake district to prove his point that a shepherd was seldom, if ever, seen without a Collie at his heels:

A tourist asked a native how many people attended a picturesque little church he was visiting. "Why," came the reply, "T'last Sunday that war ten cur dogs liggin' in 't porch an' the churchyard." From this, the questioner inferred that there were ten churchgoers since each would be attended by his sheepdog or "cur" as the Collie was locally called.

In those days obviously, the only thing wanted was a dog of excellence as a working dog, whether as a hunter, a shepherd dog, or as a watchdog, and selection would have been made only on that basis. Certainly it was not until the mid-eighteen hundreds that any attention was paid to the looks of the dog. It was in Birmingham in 1860 that the first show was held which catered to sheepdogs. J.H. Walsh, well-known authority on the dog who was later to write a number of books and magazine articles using the pseudonym of "Stonehenge," was one of the judges. There were only five entries, but one can assume that this was the first time that any of the progenitors of our present day Collie appeared in

COLLIE TALES

To prove the breed's cleverness, Rawdon Lee tells of a performing troupe of Collies he once saw in London. After going through the usual routine of circus dog tricks, one of them pushed a ladder onto the stage. This was placed against the wall of a burning house. The Collie climbed the ladder, crawled through a window and returned

Collies have been famous throughout history for their devotion to their masters as well as the children with whom they are associated. There are many stories about their bravery and the devotion of Collies to their human masters.

the show ring. Ten years later, at a later show in Birmingham, there were still only 15 entries but among them was a Old Cockie, a dog who was to become famous in Collie history as the founder of a proud line. Charlemange, perhaps the most successful of all 19th Century Champions, was his grandson. Even today, there are Collies with Cockie's blood in their veins.

with a "baby" in its mouth which he carried to a place of safety. The dog then fell over on its side, pretending to be exhausted. Two other Collies appeared pulling and pushing an ambulance and carried the "dead" dog away on a stretcher.

There is another story about a Collie who could play Nap, a common card game of the time; he was so proficient as to be able

Collies are so intelligent that they are very common in circus and movie routines. The most famous routine is a Collie climbing a ladder and entering a burning house to save a child.

Collies have been used for herding sheep in the U.K. and Europe, and for herding ostrich in South Africa. Ostriches have been known to attack a man while he attempted to herd them, but they never attack a Collie!

to hold his own with anyone his owner challenged. Apparently, however, the dog knew which cards to play by a secret signal from his master.

We read that Collies were once used in South Africa by ostrich breeders to drive the birds from "kraal to camp" for plucking their feathers. The dogs handled their unusual charges proficiently and although the great birds would frequently charge a man when angry they were cowed by the presence of the Collies.

A black Collie named Help collected for a charitable fund on the railroads of the period. On his collar was inscribed, "I am Help, the Railway Dog of England, and Travelling Agent for the Orphans of the Railway Men Killed on Duty." The contributions he collected, it is claimed, were "incredible."

Queen Victoria was the proud possessor of a white Collie, which was rare then, and still is, comparatively. Collie fanciers of the time were afraid it would start a fad for White Collies but apparently their fears were unfounded.

There are four recognized colors for Collies, namely, *sable and white, tricolor, blue merle* (shown here) and *white.*

THE COLLIE IN AMERICA

In common with Collies everywhere, the American Collie of today owes his origin to his British forebears, and a debt to the American fanciers who so assiduously made raids on the home country and purchased some of the very best British stock.

The first American dog show was held in Philadelphia in 1877, but no Collies appear to have been exhibited. The first record of Collies at an American show was in the following year, at Westminster where as in Britain they competed in classes for Sheepdogs.

Interest in the breed grew during the next decade, each show having more exhibits than the previous one, until, in 1886, the Collie Club of America came into being. As you know, it is still with us, and thus is one of the oldest breed clubs of any breed anywhere in the world.

Throughout this decade Collie fanciers repeatedly imported stock from across the

Atlantic, and competition became more and more keen, while the breeding of Collies grew both in numbers and in interest. Imports during this time included such dogs as Tweed II, Ayrshire Laddie, Marcus, Ch. Dublin Scot and Ch. Flurry II to mention only a few of those names are still to be found behind today's pedigrees.

where Collies are discussed—came into being: the Chestnut Hills of Mr. Mitchell Harrison, Wellesbourne, which had started in England and which now came over, dogs, kennel name, kennel manager and all; Mr. J.P. Morgan's Cargstons; the Coilas or Mr. Ormiston Roy; Brandane (Messers Black and Hunter); and Imna of Miss Bullocke, to mention

Three different Collie colors. The color of the Collie has no influence over the Collie's temperament, intelligence, size or quality.

1894 was a near golden year for the breed in America, for it was at this moment that Ch. Christopher, Ch. Sefton Hero and Charlton Phyllis left Britain For this country.

During the latter years of the last, and early years of this century many of the kennel names—household words today

only a few. All these owners imported many specimens, some of them going to the length of returning their bitches to Britain to be bred, returning again to the States before whelping—one of the reasons why pedigrees between the two countries are so inextricably mixed! Remember, of course, that this was in the days before Britain found it necessary to introduce anti-rabies quarantine restrictions.

The year 1905 saw the arrival on the scene of Mrs. Lunt's Alsteads, and a few years later the ranks were swelled by Dr. O.P. Bennett's Tazewells, Hertzvilles (Mr. H.L. Hertz) and, for a short time, the Knocklaydes of Mr. T.P. Hunter, who imported the English otherwise have left their native land.

History was to repeat itself in 1939, though it cannot be said that the Collies imported at that time made any spectacular contribution to the American fancy, by then very well established in its own particularly successful bloodlines.

All Collies, everywhere in the

Collie blood lines are established by breeding for certain qualities. Usually the qualities by which Collies are judged are those which appear in the breed standards issued by the various national clubs.

Champion Weardale Lord, renaming him Knocklayde King Hector, under which name he readily became a champion in his country of adoption and also made a name for himself as a sire.

The coming of the Great War in 1914 certainly made available to the American Market a number of top class Collies who might not world today, owe their inception to Ch. Trefoil who, whelped in 1873, is behind every one of today's Collies.

Five generations from Trefoil comes Ch. Christopher (1887) and through his two sons, Ch. Stracathro Ralph and the Edgbaston Marvel, we trace American Collie history today.

From the former came Ch. Anfield Model, a much lauded import who, excelling in many show points, particularly in head qualities, failed to pass on and was a near "flop" as a stud dog. However, Stracathro Ralph, through his son, Heather Ralph, was responsible for eleven generations later for Ch. Magnet,

The
COLLIE
ANNA KATHERINE NICHOLAS

115 Exciting
Full-Color Photos

THE COLLIE is a wonderful book that gives a complete history, breeding, and training. THE COLLIE is available through most pet shops.

to whom can be traced the major portion of top winning collies today in the USA, Europe, and Britain. Christopher's other son, Edgbaston Marvel, gave the breed four generations later Ch. Parbold Piccolo, sire of Ch. Anfield Model, but of much greater significance was his other son, Parbold Pierrot, who had a much greater influence on the breed.

To Piccolo today we trace the Bellhavens and their direct descendants, but to the Ch. Magnet line we can trace almost all the top winners in the American show ring of this decade. Through Ch. Laund Legislator we get the Lodestones, Hertzvilles, Hazeljanes, Noranda and some of the Brandywynes. But it is the other line, through Ch. Poplar Perfection's son Ch. Eden (later Alstead) Emerald that carries the main part of today's American Collie History: Brandwyne, Alstead, Sterling, Honeybrook, Starberry, Accalia, Silver-Ho, Paradere, Tokalon, Erin's Own, Royal Rock and Glenhill, to mention only a few of today's top kennels.

It really seems quite amazing that Magnet should have had such a very great influence as a sire in America, for he was already nine years of age before he reached these shores and one would have expected that his greatest days as sire were over, especially, since he had been widely used as a sire in Britain before he left and it is most interesting to note that the vast majority of winners in Britain today are also direct Magnet descendants, again through Ch. Poplar Perfection.

No Collie history would be complete without the mention of Albert Payson Terhune, whose famed "Sunnybank" stories in the 1920s did so much to popularize the breed. Nor will any of us ever forget Lassie, the beloved star of screen and television. The original Lassie was, as is now common

The Collie owes much of its popularity to the screen star named *Lassie*, which charmed millions on television and cinema. Reruns of these productions can be viewed today on late-night shows.

White Collies are rare and they are usually not all white.

gossip, a female impersonator named Pal, engaged after many auditions to play the role of "Lassie" in the picture of that name based on Eric Knight's touching story of a Collie separated from her beloved master.

Pal, according to his owner and trainer, Rudd Weatherwax, was the runt of his litter, and was never "Show" quality, although he came from good parentage. He was born in 1940, sired by Red Brucie of Glamis.

But long before Lassie, there was another Collie movie star—real name Blair, stage name Rover. Blair appeared in "Rescued by Rover" in 1905, the story of a Collie who saves a baby from kidnappers. So successful was this seven-minute drama that it led to three sequels, "Rover Drives a Car," "Baby's Playmate," and "Dumb Comrade."

The history of the Collie is by no means concluded and you who are reading these lines may well have your part to play. If so, one hopes that it will be played with as much dedication, patience and sacrifice as was evidenced by those who have gone before and by their travail made our paths easier.

DESCRIPTION OF THE COLLIE

The Collie is basically a family dog—he loves people and they love him. Bred from the sheep herding dogs and farm guardians, he has a natural instinct to protect his home and, particularly, the children in his family.

The feats of Lassie in the movies and on television are not beyond those which many Collies perform day by day in their homes. It is not by chance that Collies have been represented more often than any other breed among the winners and finalists of the dog hero awards.

The Collie is a good companion for children and adults alike, for the breed is gentle, yet playful and affectionate. As a watch dog his bark is worse than his seldom-used bite. He can be trained to be quiet and, although naturally full of bounce, to behave well indoors—even in a small apartment. The Collie is equally at home on the farm and in the city,

Lassie, the screen star, is probably the world's most famous and beloved of all dogs.

since he is happy whenever he is with "his" family.

Although often called by various names including "Scotch" or "English," "short-nosed" or "long-nosed," "Lassie-type," "Show" or "Farm" Collie, there is only one breed common in America, and that is the Collie, without any additional names.

TYPES OF COLLIES

There are two varieties, of which the Rough (or longhaired) is most often seen, and is among the most popular breeds, currently ranked among the top 50 in American Kennel Club registrations. The smooth Collie is rare and just beginning to gain favor. Since its short, dense coat does not require the care a long-coated dog should have to look its best, the Smooth will undoubtedly win popularity as a pet and guide dog for the blind. In either coat, there is no more magnificent dog than the Collie.

The Border Collie is a separate breed, probably descending from much the same type of working sheepdogs as the Collie ancestors. As a one-man working dog, the Border Collie is probably unsurpassed in intelligence. However, he is reserved and high strung, being bred as a companion for the shepherd in his lonely life, and not as a house pet. This breed is smaller than the Collie, and has

Although this Collie is mostly black, there is no such thing as a *black* Collie. The standard of the breed recognizes a *tri-color* Collie, which is mostly black.

There are two types of Collies. The Rough Collie has long hair while the Smooth Collie has a short, dense coat.

a coat of only medium length, generally black with some white markings or ticking, and rarely marked with tan. The Border Collie is commonly employed as a stock dog, and performs well in working trials. Many Border Collies work on farms, herding cattle and swine or poultry as well as sheep. The Bearded Collie has its own breed club in England. It is a shaggy, bob-tailed breed similar to the Old English Sheepdog, which is probably a descendant of the Scottish bearded working Collies of centuries ago.

The Shetland Sheepdog, often called a miniature Collie, is actually a small version of the full-sized breed. The "Sheltie," as it is often called, was developed as a yard and sheep dog in the barren Shetland Islands, north of Scotland, as its name implies. Like the ponies which also bear the name of the islands, Shetland sheep are small, and so a large sheep dog was not needed to guard the flocks.

The name "Farm Collie" is particularly popular, although there is no recognized breed by that name. It could be characterized as a group of dogs of collie type, more or less alike, with the short nose and moderate coat of today's Collie's ancestors. These dogs may be tan with black markings or in the same colors as the Collie, to which they are to some degree related. The

A Collie (the larger of the two dogs) and a Shetland Sheepdog, often called a *Sheltie*. While they have outward similarities, a close examination indicates major differences from a breed standard point of view.

The faces of a tricolor (black) and blue merle are differently marked.

belief that these dogs are more intelligent than the longer-nosed, aristocratic-looking show-dog Collies has little foundation. There are "dumb" dogs in any breed, but dogs which are bred for intelligence as well as looks are as smart as any mongrel—and smarter than most. Several kennels which produce top quality show winners also sell dogs which are *outstanding* obedience performers or working farm dogs. With a dog of known back-ground you have some guarantee of his future. There are no rules for registering these "farm collies," and no controlling organization, so breeding is not selective, and you cannot be sure that your puppy will resemble his parents.

Three color varieties of Smooth Collies.

STANDARD FOR THE BREED

A breed standard is the criterion by which the appearance (and to a certain extent, the temperament as well) of any given dog is made subject to objective measurement. Basically, the standard for any breed is a definition of the perfect dog, to which all specimens of the breed are compared. Breed standards are always subject to change through review by the national breed club for each dog, so it is always wise to keep up with developments in a breed by checking the publications of your national kennel club.

A beautiful blue merle Collie, like this one, may have good looks, but when judged according to the standard, basic *good looks* alone won't win.

OFFICIAL AKC STANDARD FOR THE COLLIE

General Appearance—The Collie is a lithe, strong, responsive, active dog, carrying no useless timber, standing naturally straight and firm. The deep, moderately wide chest shows strength, the sloping shoulders and well-bent hocks indicate speed and grace, and the face shows high intelligence. The Collie presents an impressive, proud picture of true balance, each part being in harmonious proportion to every other part and to the whole. Except for the technical description that is essential to this Standard and without which no standard for the guidance of breeders and judges is adequate, it could be stated simply that no part of the Collie ever seems to be out of proportion to any other part. Timidity, frailness, sullenness, viciousness, lack of animation, cumbersome appearance and lack of overall balance impair the general character.

Head—The head properties are of great importance. When considered in proportion to the

The Collie champion, like this specimen, is judged by many factors such as those labelled below. In general appearance, the breed is lithe, strong, responsive, active, slim and stands straight and firm.

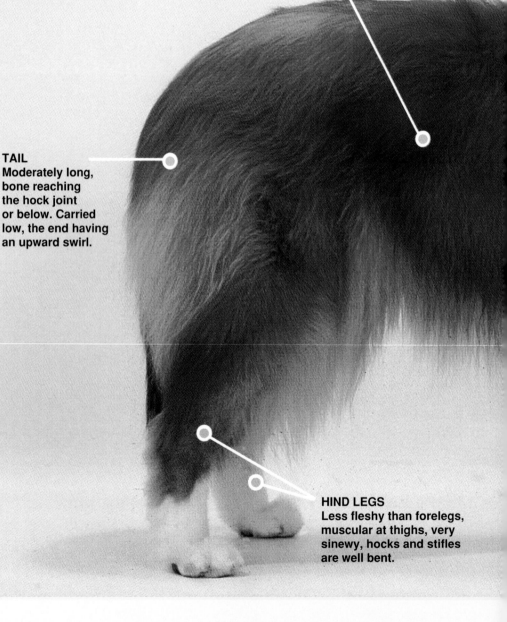

BODY
Firm, hard and muscular, a trifle long in proportion to the height. Ribs well rounded; chest is deep.

TAIL
Moderately long, bone reaching the hock joint or below. Carried low, the end having an upward swirl.

HIND LEGS
Less fleshy than forelegs, muscular at thighs, very sinewy, hocks and stifles are well bent.

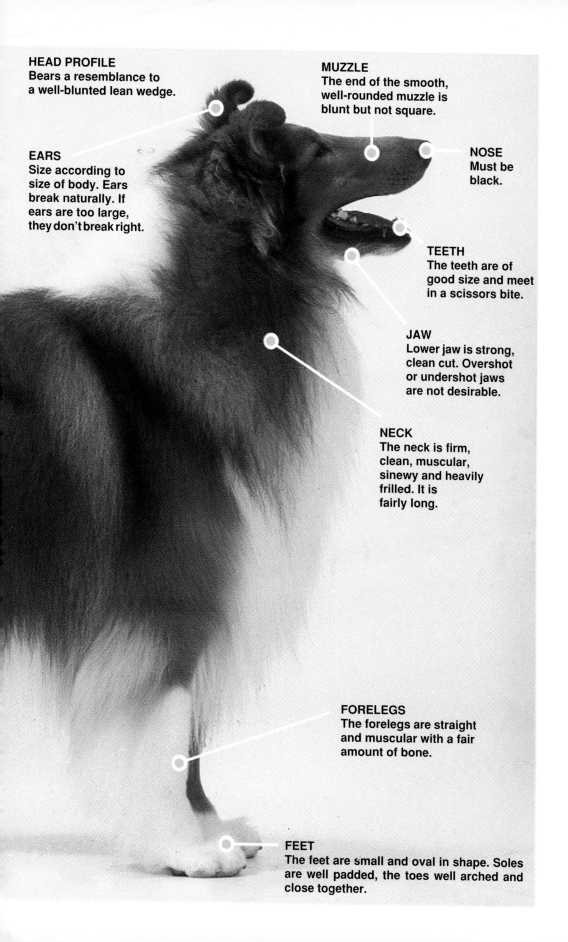

HEAD PROFILE
Bears a resemblance to
a well-blunted lean wedge.

MUZZLE
The end of the smooth,
well-rounded muzzle is
blunt but not square.

NOSE
Must be
black.

EARS
Size according to
size of body. Ears
break naturally. If
ears are too large,
they don't break right.

TEETH
The teeth are of
good size and meet
in a scissors bite.

JAW
Lower jaw is strong,
clean cut. Overshot
or undershot jaws
are not desirable.

NECK
The neck is firm,
clean, muscular,
sinewy and heavily
frilled. It is
fairly long.

FORELEGS
The forelegs are straight
and muscular with a fair
amount of bone.

FEET
The feet are small and oval in shape. Soles
are well padded, the toes well arched and
close together.

size of the dog, the head is inclined to lightness and never appears massive. A heavy-headed dog lacks the necessary bright, alert, full-of-sense look that contributes so greatly to expression. Both in front and profile view, the head bears a general resemblance to a well-blunted lean wedge, being smooth and clean in outline and nicely balanced in proportion. On the sides it tapers gradually and smoothly from the ears to the end of the black nose, without being flared out in backskull ("cheeky") or pinched in muzzle ("snipy"). In profile view the top of the backskull and the top of the muzzle lie in two approximately parallel, straight planes of equal length, divided by a very slight but perceptible stop or break. A mid-point between the inside corners of the eyes (which is the center of a correctly placed stop) is the center of balance in length of head.

The end of the smooth, well-rounded muzzle is blunt but not square. The underjaw is strong, clean-cut and the depth of skull from the brow to the under part of the jaw is not excessive. The teeth are of good size, meeting in a scissors bite. *Overshot or undershot jaws are undesirable, the latter being more severely penalized.* There is a very slight prominence of the eyebrows. The backskull is flat, without receding either laterally or backward and the occipital

PROFILES OF THE COLLIE

Correct head
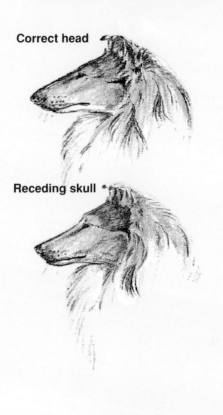

Receding skull

Roman nose and overshot

Dish-faced
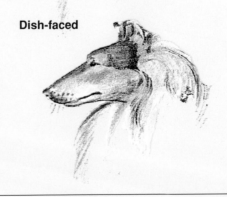

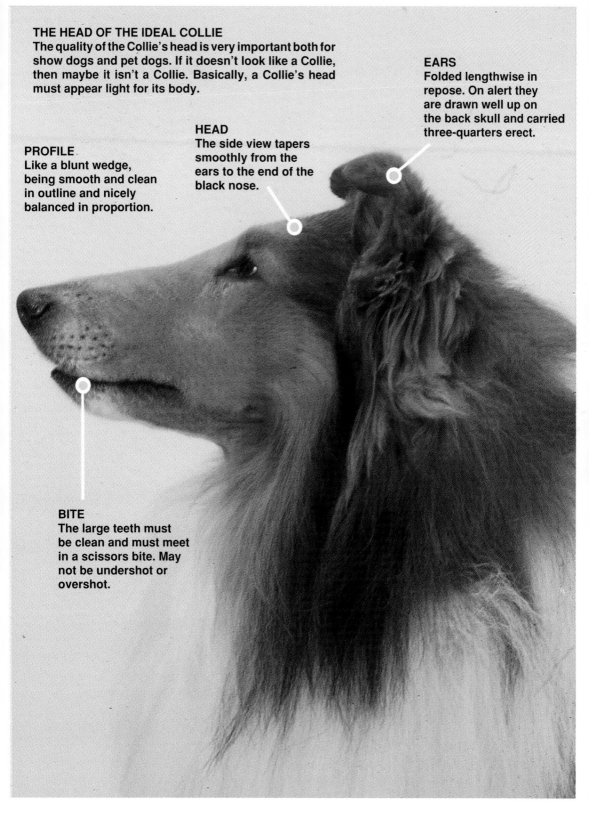

THE HEAD OF THE IDEAL COLLIE
The quality of the Collie's head is very important both for show dogs and pet dogs. If it doesn't look like a Collie, then maybe it isn't a Collie. Basically, a Collie's head must appear light for its body.

EARS
Folded lengthwise in repose. On alert they are drawn well up on the back skull and carried three-quarters erect.

HEAD
The side view tapers smoothly from the ears to the end of the black nose.

PROFILE
Like a blunt wedge, being smooth and clean in outline and nicely balanced in proportion.

BITE
The large teeth must be clean and must meet in a scissors bite. May not be undershot or overshot.

bone is not highly peaked. The proper width of backskull is less than its length. Thus the correct width varies with the individual and is dependent upon the extent to which it is supported by length of muzzle. Because of the importance of the head characteristics, *prominent head faults are very severely penalized.*

Eyes—Because of the combination of the flat skull, the arched eyebrows, the slight stop and the rounded muzzle, the foreface must be chiseled to form a receptacle for the eyes and they are necessarily placed obliquely to give them the required forward outlook. Except for the blue merles, they are required to be matched in color. They are almond-shaped, of medium size and never properly appear to be large or prominent. The color is dark and the eye does not show a yellow ring or a sufficiently prominent haw to affect the dog's expression. The eyes have a clear, bright appearance, expressing intelligent inquisitiveness, particularly when the ears are drawn up and the dog is on the alert. In blue merles, dark brown eyes are preferable, but either or both eyes may be merle or china in color without specific penalty. A large, round, full eye seriously detracts from the desired "sweet" expression. *Eye faults are heavily penalized.*

Ears—The ears are in proportion to the size of the head and, if they are carried properly and unquestionably "break" naturally, are seldom too small. Large ears usually cannot be lifted correctly off the head, and even if lifted, they will be out of proportion to the size of the head. When in repose the ears are folded lengthwise and thrown back into the frill. On the alert they are drawn well up on the backskull and carried about three-quarters erect, with about one-fourth of the ear tipping or "breaking" forward. *A dog with prick ears or low ears cannot show true expression and is penalized accordingly.*

Neck—The neck is firm, clean, muscular, sinewy and heavily frilled. It is fairly long, carried upright with a slight arch at the nape and imparts a proud, upstanding appearance showing off the frill.

Body—The body is firm, hard and muscular, a trifle long in proportion to the height. The ribs are well-rounded behind the well-sloped shoulders and the chest is deep, extending to the elbows. The back is strong and level, supported by powerful hips and thighs and the croup is sloped to give a well-rounded finish. The loin is powerful and slightly arched. *Noticeably fat dogs, or dogs in poor flesh, or with skin disease, or with no undercoat are out of condition and are moderately penalized accordingly.*

Legs—The forelegs are straight and muscular, with a fair amount of bone considering the size of the dog. A cumbersome appearance is undesirable. *Both narrow and wide placement are penalized.* The forearm is moderately fleshy and the pasterns are flexible but without weakness. The hind legs

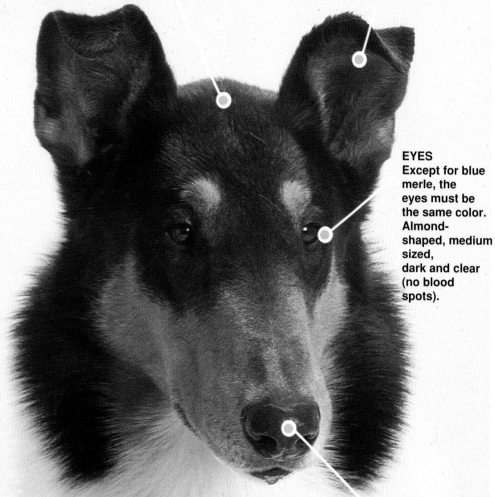

HEAD
Head is inclined
to lightness and
never appears
massive.

EARS
A Collie cannot have
prick ears or low ears.

EYES
Except for blue
merle, the
eyes must be
the same color.
Almond-
shaped, medium
sized,
dark and clear
(no blood
spots).

NOSE
Black and clean.
Must not have
discharge of
any type.

NECK
Firm, smooth, clean,
muscular, sinewy and
heavily frilled.

THE FACE OF THE COLLIE
A good Collie must have a bright, alert,
full-of-sense look that contributes so
greatly to expression.

are less fleshy, muscular at the thighs, very sinewy and the hocks and stifles are well bent. *A cowhocked dog or a dog with straight stifles is penalized.* The comparatively small feet are approximately oval in shape. The soles are well padded and tough, and the toes are well arched and close together. When the Collie is not in motion, the legs and feet are judged by allowing the dog to come to a natural stop in a standing position so that both the forelegs and the hind legs are placed well apart, with the feet extending straight forward. Excessive "posing" is undesirable.

Gait—Gait is sound. When the dog is moved at a slow trot toward an observer its straight front legs track comparatively close together at the ground. The front legs are not out at the elbows, do not "cross over," nor does the dog move with a choppy, rolling or pacing gait. When viewed from the rear the hind legs are straight, tracking comparatively close together at the ground. At a moderate trot the hind legs are powerful and propelling. Viewed from the side the reasonably long, "reaching" stride is smooth and even, keeping the back line firm and level.

As the speed of the gait is increased the Collie single tracks, bringing the front legs inward in a straight line from the shoulder toward the center line of the body and the hind legs inward in a straight line from the hip toward the center line of the body. The gait suggests effortless speed combined with the dog's herding heritage, requiring it to be capable of changing its direction of travel almost instantaneously.

Tail—The tail is moderately long, the bone reaching to the hock joint or below. It is carried low when the dog is quiet, the end having an upward twist or "swirl." When gaited or when the dog is excited it is carried gaily but not over the back.

Coat— Rough—The well-fitting, proper-textured coat is the crowning glory of the rough variety of Collie. It is abundant except on the head and legs. The outer coat is straight and harsh to the touch. *A soft, open outer coat or a curly outer coat, regardless of quantity is penalized.* The undercoat, however, is soft, furry and so close together that it is difficult to see the skin when the hair is parted. The coat is very abundant on the mane and frill. The face or mask is smooth. The forelegs are smooth and well feathered to the back of the pasterns. The hind legs are smooth below the hock joints. Any feathering below the hocks is removed for the show ring. The hair on the tail is very profuse and on the hips it is long and bushy. The texture, quantity and the extent to which the coat "fits the dog" are important points. **Smooth**—The smooth variety of Collie is judged by the same Standard as the rough variety except that the references to the quantity and the distribution of the coat are not applicable to the smooth variety, which has a short, hard, dense, flat coat of good texture, with an abundance of undercoat.

THE SMOOTH COLLIE
It is judged by the same standard as as the Rough Collie except for the references to coat quantity and distribution. Dogs should reach from 24 to 26 inches at the shoulder and weigh 60 to 75 pounds. Bitches should reach 22 to 24 inches at the shoulder and weigh 50 to 65 pounds. Collies that are too large or too small are penalized by judges at dog shows.

♀
24"- 26"

♂
22"- 24"

Collies are measured from the shoulders (withers) to the ground.

THE COLLIE FROM THE FRONT

Correct front

Out at elbow and pin-toed.

Too wide and heavy in front.

Too narrow in front and the toes are turned out.

THE COLLIE FROM THE REAR

Correct hocks

Cow Hocks

Hocks too wide

Narrow Hindquarters

Expression is one of the most important points in considering the value of Collies, both from a professional, dog-show point of view and from a sales appeal, commercial point of view.

Color—The four recognized colors are "Sable and White," "Tri-Color," "Blue Merle," and "White." There is no preference among them. The "Sable and White" is predominantly sable (a fawn sable color of varying shades from light gold to dark mahogany) with white markings usually on the chest, neck, legs, feet and the tip of the tail. A blaze may appear on the foreface or on the backskull or both. The "Tri-Color" is predominantly black, carrying white markings as in a "Sable and White" and has tan shadings on and about the head and legs. The "Blue Merle" is a mottled or "marbled" color predominantly blue-gray and black with white markings as in the "Sable and White"and usually has tan shadings as in the "Tri-Color." The "White" is predominantly white, preferably with sable, tri-color or blue merle markings.

Size—Dogs are from 24 to 26 inches at the shoulder and weigh from 60 to 75 pounds. Bitches are from 22 to 24 inches at the shoulder, weighing from 50 to 65 pounds. *An undersize or oversize Collie is penalized according to the extent to which the dog appears to be undersize or oversize.*

Expression—Expression is one of the most important points in considering the relative value of Collies. *Expression* like the term "character" is difficult to define in words. It is not a fixed point like color, weight or height and it is something the uninitiated can properly understand only by optical illustration. In general, however, it may be said to be the combined product of shape and balance of the skull and muzzle, the placement, size, shape and color of the eye and the position, size and carriage of the ears. An expression that shows sullenness or which is suggestive of any other breed is entirely foreign. The Collie cannot be judged properly until its expression has been carefully evaluated.

When selecting your new Collie puppy, you are advised to let the Collie puppy select YOU. Stand in front of a group of puppies and see which one comes to you first! You can hardly go wrong using this method of puppy selection.

YOUR NEW COLLIE PUPPY

SELECTION

When you do pick out a Collie puppy as a pet, don't be hasty; the longer you study puppies, the better you will understand them. Make it your transcendent concern to select only one that radiates good health and spirit and is lively on his feet, whose eyes are bright, whose coat shines, and who comes forward eagerly to make and to cultivate your acquaintance. Don't fall for any shy little darling that wants to retreat to his bed or his box, or plays coy behind other puppies or people, or hides his head under your arm or jacket appealing to your protective instinct. *Pick the Collie puppy who forthrightly picks you! The feeling of attraction should be mutual!*

Puppies must chew on safe toys. They also need nutrition. The product CHOOZ serves both purposes for the Collie puppy. It is highly nutritious with about a 75% protein content and it is very hard so the puppy satisfies his chewing instincts. This also aids the Collie puppy in the proper development of his teeth and jaw muscles.

DOCUMENTS

Now, a little paper work is in order. When you purchase a purebred Collie puppy, you should receive a transfer of ownership, registration material, and other "papers" (a list of the immunization shots, if any, the puppy may have been given; a note on whether or not the puppy has been wormed; a diet and feeding schedule to which the puppy is accustomed) and you are welcomed as a fellow owner to a long, pleasant association with a most lovable pet, and more (news)paper work.

GENERAL PREPARATION

You have chosen to own a particular Collie puppy. You have chosen it very carefully over all other breeds and all other puppies. So before you ever get that Collie puppy home, you will have prepared for its arrival by reading everything you can get your hands on having to do with the management of Collies and puppies. True, you will run into many conflicting opinions, but at least you will not be starting "blind." Read, study, digest. Talk over your plans with your veterinarian, other "Collie people," and the seller of your Collie puppy.

When you get your Collie puppy, you will find that your

TRANSPORTATION

If you take the puppy home by car, protect him from drafts, particularly in cold weather. Wrapped in a towel and carried in the arms or lap of a passenger, the Collie puppy will usually make the trip without mishap. If the pup starts to drool and to squirm, stop the car for a few minutes. Have newspapers handy in case of car-sickness. A covered carton lined with newspapers provides protection for puppy and car, if you are driving alone. Avoid

A pair of blue merle Collie puppies. Coming from the same parents, they can be expected to look alike. Most champion lines have been consistently bred for the production of good quality puppies. This is assured by selectively breeding for desirable characteristics. That's what dog shows and championships are all about: *producing puppies with predictable results.*

reading and study are far from finished. You've just scratched the surface in your plan to provide the greatest possible comfort and health for your Collie; and, by the same token, you do want to assure yourself of the greatest possible enjoyment of this wonderful creature. You must be ready for this puppy mentally as well as in the physical requirements.

excitement and unnecessary handling of the puppy on arrival. A Collie puppy is a very small "package" to be making a complete change of surroundings and company, he needs frequent rest and refreshment.

THE FIRST DAY AND NIGHT

When your Collie puppy arrives in your home, put him down on the floor and don't pick him up again, except when it is absolutely necessary. He is a dog, a real dog, and must not be lugged around like a rag doll. Handle him as little as possible, and permit no one to pick him up and baby him. To repeat, *put your Collie puppy on the floor or the ground and let him stay there except when it may be necessary to do otherwise.*

treatment. Be calm, friendly, and reassuring. Encourage him to walk around and sniff over his new home. If it's dark, put on the lights. Let him roam for a few minutes while you and everyone else concerned sit quietly or go about your routine business. Let the puppy come back to you.

Playmates may cause an immediate problem if the new Collie puppy is to be greeted by

It's not only important for a Collie puppy to look good, but it must move well, too. The puppy's gait is important.

Quite possibly your Collie puppy will be afraid for a while in his new surroundings, without his mother and littermates. Comfort him and reassure him, but don't console him. Don't give him the "oh-you-poor-itsy-bitsy-puppy"

children or other pets. If not, you can skip this subject. The natural affinity between puppies and children calls for some supervision until a live-and-let-live relationship is established. This applies particularly to a Christmas puppy, when there is more excitement than usual and more chance for a puppy to swallow something upsetting. It is a better plan to welcome the puppy several days before or after the holiday week. Like a baby, your Collie puppy needs much rest and should not be over-handled. Once a child realizes that a puppy has "feelings" similar to his own, and can readily be hurt or injured, the opportunities for play and responsibilities provide exercise and training for both.

For his first night with you, he should be put where he is to sleep every night—say in the kitchen, since its floor can usually be easily cleaned. Let him explore the kitchen to his heart's content; close doors to confine him there. Prepare his food and feed him lightly the first night. Give him a pan with some water in it—not a lot, since most puppies will try to drink the whole pan dry. Give him an old coat or shirt to lie on. Since a coat or shirt will be strong in human scent, he will pick it out to lie on, thus furthering his feeling of security in the room where he has just been fed.

Your new Collie puppy should have time to familiarize himself with his new surroundings. Remember to always supervise a puppy, especially when he is outdoors.

Ideally, the Collie puppy will not be alone. If you are lucky enough to buy two Collie puppies of the same age, and keep them in a large yard, you will have happy companion animals. Collies are delighted to be outside most of the time with plenty of space for running and playing.

HOUSEBREAKING HELPS

Now, sooner or later—mostly sooner—your new Collie puppy is going to "puddle" on the floor. First take a newspaper and lay it on the puddle until the urine is soaked up onto the paper. *Save this paper.* Now take a cloth with soap and water, wipe up the floor and dry it well. Then take the wet paper and place it on a fairly large square of newspapers in a convenient corner. When cleaning up, always keep a piece of wet paper on top of the others. Every time he wants to "squat," he will seek out this spot and use the papers. (This routine is rarely necessary for more than three days.) Now leave your Collie puppy for the night. Quite probably he will cry and howl a bit; some are more stubborn than others on this matter. But let him stay alone for the night. This may seem harsh treatment, but it is the best procedure in the long run. Just let him cry; he will weary of it sooner or later.

Your Collie puppy should be fed the diet available at your local pet shop. Pet shops usually have better-quality dog foods available than supermarkets.

FEEDING

Now let's talk about feeding your Collie, a subject so simple that it's amazing there is so much nonsense and misunderstanding about it. Is it expensive to feed a Collie? No, it is not! You can feed your Collie economically and keep him in perfect shape the year round, or you can feed him expensively. He'll thrive either way, and let's see why this is true.

First of all, remember a Collie is a dog. Dogs do not have a high degree of selectivity in their food, and unless you spoil them with great variety (and possibly turn them into poor, "picky" eaters) they will eat almost anything that they become accustomed to. Many dogs flatly refuse to eat nice, fresh beef. They pick around it and eat everything else. But meat—bah! Why? They aren't accustomed to it! They'd eat rabbit fast enough, but they refuse beef because they aren't used to it.

There are dozens of dog foods available. By far the best dog foods are dry in kibble, meal or pellet form.

VARIETY NOT NECESSARY

A good general rule of thumb is forget all human preferences and don't give a thought to variety. Choose the right diet for your Collie and feed it to him day after day, year after year, winter and summer. But what is the right diet?

Hundreds of thousands of dollars have been spent in canine nutrition research. The results are pretty conclusive, so you needn't go into a lot of experimenting with trials of this and that every other week. Research has proven just what your dog needs to eat and to keep healthy.

DOG FOOD

There are almost as many right diets as there are dog experts, but the basic diet most often recommended is one that consists of a dry food, either meal or kibble form. There are several of excellent quality, manufactured by reliable companies, research tested, and nationally advertised. They are inexpensive, highly satisfactory, and easily available in stores everywhere in containers of five to 50 pounds. Larger amounts cost less per pound, usually.

If you have a choice of brands, it is usually safer to choose the better known one; but even so, carefully read the analysis on the package. Do not choose any food in which the protein level is less than 25 percent, and be sure that this protein comes from both animal and vegetable sources. The good dog foods have meat meal, fish meal, liver, and such, plus protein from alfalfa and soy beans, as well as some dried-milk product. Note the vitamin content carefully. See that they are all there in good proportions; and be especially certain that the food contains properly high levels of vitamins A and D, two of the most perishable and important ones. Note the B-complex level, but don't worry about carbohydrate and mineral levels. These substances are plentiful and cheap and not likely to be lacking in a good brand.

The advice given for how to choose a dry food also applies to moist or canned types of dog foods, if you decide to feed one of these.

Having chosen a really good food, feed it to your Collie as the manufacturer directs. And once you've started, stick to it. Never change if you can possibly help it. A switch from one meal or kibble-

Don't let your Collie puppy play with your child's toys. First of all, they are probably not safe for the puppy...and the toys are usually unfit for the child once the dog has soiled it or torn it open. Your pet shop can help you with safe dog toys specifically designed for dogs like this one.

type food can usually be made without too much upset; however, a change will almost invariably give you (and your Collie) some trouble.

WHEN SUPPLEMENTS ARE NEEDED

Now what about supplements of various kinds, mineral and vitamin, or the various oils? They are all okay to add to your Collie's food. However, if you are feeding your Collie a correct diet, and this is easy to do, no supplements are necessary unless your Collie has been improperly fed, has been sick, or is having puppies. Vitamins and minerals are naturally present in all the foods; and to ensure against any loss through processing, they are added in concentrated form to the dog food you use. Except on the advice of your veterinarian, added amounts of vitamins can prove harmful to your Collie! The same risk goes with minerals.

Naturally Flavor Enhanced
NG-104 FOR LARGE DOGS
NYLABONE
SAVES MONEY & DOGS' LIVES
ENDORSED BY LEADING DOG AUTHORITIES & GUARANTEED!
... ASK YOUR VETERINARIAN
MADE IN THE USA
POOCH PACIFIER GIANT SIZE
IRRESISTIBLE TO DOGS

More than most other breeds, Collies have to chew, especially puppies, since tooth loss and gum disease in Collies are substantially high. The safest and most effective dog bones are those made by Nylabone. They are the only bones which have been tested and proven safe and effective. They have been on the market for about 40 years. They are available at all pet shops. The specimen shown here has been chewed on both ends. When the knuckles get chewed down, the bone should be replaced.

FEEDING SCHEDULE

When and how much food to give your Collie? As to when (except in the instance of puppies), suit yourself. You may feed two meals per day or the same amount in one single feeding, either morning or night. As to how to prepare the food and how much to give, it is generally best to follow the directions on the food package. Your own Collie may want a little more or a little less.

Fresh, cool water should always be available to your Collie. This is important to good health throughout his lifetime.

ALL COLLIES NEED TO CHEW

Puppies and young Collies need something with resistance to chew on while their teeth and jaws are developing—for cutting the puppy teeth, to induce growth of the permanent teeth under the puppy teeth, to assist in getting rid of the puppy teeth at the proper time, to help the permanent teeth through the gums, to ensure normal jaw development, and to settle the permanent teeth solidly in the jaws.

The adult Collie's desire to chew stems from the instinct for tooth cleaning, gum massage, and jaw exercise—plus the need for an outlet for periodic doggie tensions.

This is why dogs, especially puppies and young dogs, will often destroy property worth hundreds of dollars when their chewing instinct is not diverted from their owner's possessions. And this is why you should provide your Collie with something to chew—something that has the necessary functional qualities, is desirable from the Collie's viewpoint, and is safe for him.

It is very important that your Collie not be permitted to chew on anything he can break or on any indigestible thing from which he can bite sizable chunks. Sharp pieces, such as from a bone which can be broken by a dog, may pierce the intestinal wall and kill.

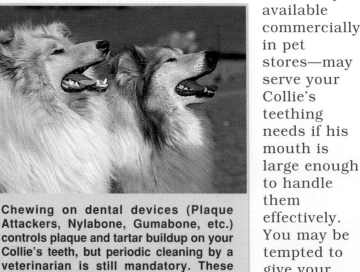

Chewing on dental devices (Plaque Attackers, Nylabone, Gumabone, etc.) controls plaque and tartar buildup on your Collie's teeth, but periodic cleaning by a veterinarian is still mandatory. These Collies are showing off their pearly whites.

Indigestible things that can be bitten off in chunks, such as from shoes or rubber or plastic toys, may cause an intestinal stoppage (if not regurgitated) and bring painful death, unless surgery is promptly performed.

Strong natural bones, such as 4- to 8-inch lengths of round shin bone from mature beef—either the kind you can get from a butcher or one of the variety available commercially in pet stores—may serve your Collie's teething needs if his mouth is large enough to handle them effectively. You may be tempted to give your Collie puppy a smaller bone and he may not be able to break it when you do, but puppies grow rapidly and the power of their jaws constantly increases until maturity. This means that a growing Collie may break one of the smaller bones at any time, swallow the pieces, and die painfully before you realize what is wrong.

All hard natural bones are very abrasive. If your Collie is an avid chewer, natural bones may wear away his teeth prematurely; hence, they then should be taken away from your dog when the teething purposes have been served. The badly worn, and usually painful, teeth of many mature dogs can be traced to excessive chewing on natural bones.

Contrary to popular belief, knuckle bones that can be chewed up and swallowed by your Collie provide little, if any, usable calcium or other nutriment. They do, however, disturb the digestion of most dogs and cause them to vomit the nourishing food they need.

Dried rawhide products of various types, shapes, sizes, and prices are available on the market and have become quite popular. However, they don't serve the primary chewing functions very well; they are a bit messy when wet from

Nylon knotted ropes are ideal for the Collie to chew on. As his teeth go into the strands of the nylon, they act as dental floss. To make them even more effective, play tug with your Collie and allow the nylon strands to be pulled through his teeth as the self-lubricating nylon slowly slides out of the Collie's grip. *Do NOT use cotton ropes as they are organic, support bacterial growth, are weak and tear easily.* You never see human dental flosses made of cotton, so why buy one for your dog?

mouthing, and most Collies chew them up rather rapidly—but they have been considered safe for dogs until recently. Now, more and more incidents of death, and near death, by strangulation have been reported to be the results of partially swallowed chunks of rawhide swelling in the throat. More recently, some veterinarians have been attributing cases of acute constipation to large pieces of incompletely digested rawhide in the intestine.

A new product, molded rawhide, is very safe. During the process, the rawhide is melted and then injection molded into the familiar dog shape. It is very hard and is eagerly accepted by Collies. The melting process also sterilizes the rawhide. Don't confuse this with

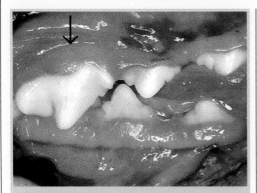

In a scientific study, this shows a dog's tooth (arrow) while being maintained by Gumabone® chewing.

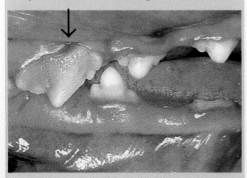

The Gumabone® was taken away and in 30 days the tooth was almost completely covered with plaque and tartar.

cleaning and vigorous gum massage, much in the same way your toothbrush does it for you. The little projections are raked off and swallowed in the form of thin shavings, but the chemistry of the nylon is such that they break down in the stomach fluids and pass through without effect.

The toughness of the nylon provides the strong chewing resistance needed for important jaw exercise and effectively aids teething functions, but there is no tooth wear because nylon is non-abrasive. Being inert, nylon does not support the growth of microorganisms; and it can be washed in soap and water or it

The nylon tug toy is actually dental floss. These nylon toys can be thrown into the washing machine when they become soiled. They come in several sizes, so get the largest as Collies love to play with these devices

pressed rawhide, which is nothing more than small strips of rawhide squeezed together.

The nylon bones, especially those with natural meat and bone fractions added, are probably the most complete, safe, and economical answer to the chewing need. Dogs cannot break them or bite off sizable chunks; hence, they are completely safe—and being longer lasting than other things offered for the purpose, they are economical.

Hard chewing raises little bristle-like projections on the surface of the nylon bones—to provide effective interim tooth

Most pet shops have complete departments dedicated to safe pacifiers for Collies, both adults and puppies.

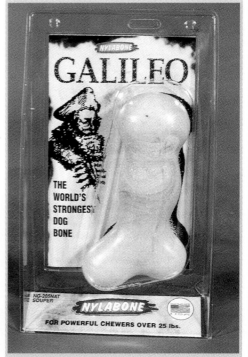

The Galileo is an extremely tough nylon pacifier. Its design is based upon original sketches by Galileo. A booklet explaining the history and workings of the design come inside each package. This might really be the best chew device and tartar controller for Collies.

Collies have such strong jaws that most ordinary pacifiers (chew devices) are quickly destroyed. The Hercules has been designed with Collies in mind. The Hercules is made of semi-elastic polyurethane, like some car bumpers.

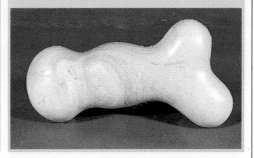

Raised dental tips on each dog bone works wonders with controlling plaque in a Collie.

Only get the largest plaque attacker for your Collie.

can be sterilized by boiling or in an autoclave.

Nylabone® is highly recommended by veterinarians as a safe, healthy nylon bone that can't splinter or chip. Nylabone® is frizzled by the dog's chewing action, creating a toothbrush-like surface that cleanses the teeth and massages the gums. Nylabone®, the only chew strongest and longest-lasting type of nylon available. The cheaper bones are made from recycled or re-ground nylon scraps, and have a tendency to break apart and split easily.

Nothing, however, substitutes for periodic professional attention for your Collie's teeth and gums, not any more than your toothbrush can do that for you.

Almost the worst thing you can allow your Collie to chew on is a dead branch. The bark may be poisonous, it may have been contaminated with another dog's urine and could pass on any one of a dozen diseases and parasites, and it's dangerous as the Collie might get a splinter in its mouth or even swallow a piece and choke.

products made of flavor-impregnated solid nylon, are available in your local pet shop. Nylabone® is superior to the cheaper bones because it is made of virgin nylon, which is the

Have your Collie's teeth cleaned at least once a year by your veterinarian (twice a year is better) and he will be happier, healthier, and far more pleasant to live with.

TRAINING

You owe proper training to your Collie. The right and privilege of being trained is his birthright; and whether your Collie is going to be a handsome, well-mannered housedog and companion, a show dog, or whatever possible use he may be put to, the basic training is always the same—all must start with basic obedience, or what might be called "manner training."

Your Collie must come instantly when called and obey the "Sit" or "Down" command just as fast; he must walk quietly at

Training your Collie is a necessity. If you have neither the will nor the time to train your Collie, you shouldn't have bought one in the first place!

"Heel," whether on or off lead. He must be mannerly and polite wherever he goes; he must be polite to strangers on the street and in stores. He must be mannerly in the presence of other dogs. He must not bark at children on roller skates, motorcycles, or other domestic animals. And he must be restrained from chasing cats. It is not a dog's inalienable right to chase cats, and he must be reprimanded for it.

PROFESSIONAL TRAINING

How do you go about this training? Well, it's a very simple procedure, pretty well standardized by now. First, if you can afford the extra expense, you may send your Collie to a professional trainer, where in 30 to 60 days he will learn how to be a "good dog." If you enlist the services of a good professional trainer, follow his advice of when to come to see the dog. No, he won't forget you, but too-frequent visits at the wrong time may slow down his training progress. And using a "pro" trainer means that you will have to go for some training, too, after the trainer feels your Collie is ready to go home. You will have to learn how your Collie works, just what to expect of him and how to use what the dog has learned after he is home.

OBEDIENCE TRAINING CLASS

Another way to train your Collie (many experienced Collie people think this is the best) is to join an obedience training class right in your own community. There is such a group in nearly every community nowadays. Here you will be working with a group of people who are also just starting out. You will actually be training your own dog, since all work is done under the direction of a head trainer who will make suggestions to you and also tell you when and how to correct your Collie's errors. Then, too, working with such a group, your Collie will learn to get along with other dogs. And, what is more important, he will learn to do exactly what he is told to do, no matter how much

SUCCESSFUL DOG TRAINING is one of the better books by which you can train your Collie. The author, Michael Kamer, trains dogs for Hollywood stars and movies.

Your Collie must be trained to COME when called. Obeying the COME command is necessary for safety.

confusion there is around him or how great the temptation is to go his own way.

Write to your national kennel club for the location of a training club or class in your locality. Sign up. Go to it regularly—every session! Go early and leave late! Both you and your Collie will benefit tremendously.

TRAIN HIM BY THE BOOK

The third way of training your Collie is by the book. Yes, you can do it this way and do a good job of it too. But in using the book method, select a book, buy it, study it carefully; then study it some more, until the procedures are almost second nature to you. Then start your training. But stay with the book and its advice and exercises. Don't start in and then

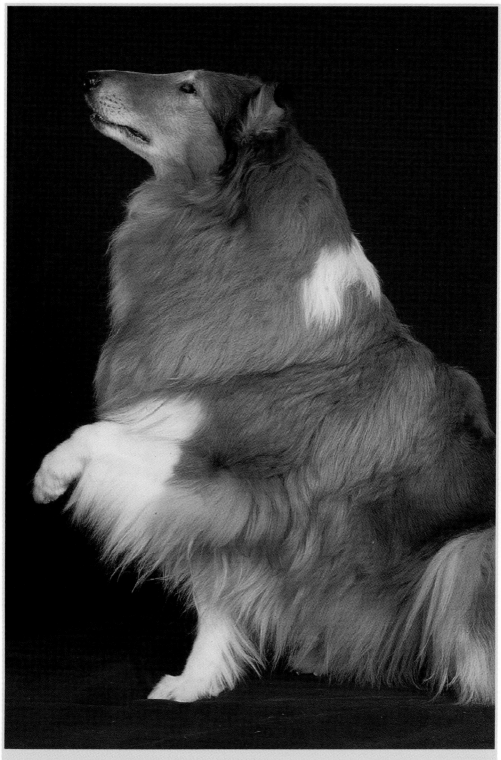

GIVE ME YOUR PAW is a charming, though meaningless command. More important would be such commands as COME, SIT or DOWN.

You can also teach your Collie to obey hand signals. This Collie has obeyed a DOWN hand signal.

Special Frisbees®* are available with a bone molded on top so the Collie can grip it should it land on a flat surface. These Frisbees®* are made especially for dogs out of nylon or Gumabone tough polyurethane.

Chasing and catching a Frisbee®* is a safe sport providing you play with your Collie away from streets or other dangerous areas.

Collies are naturally playful. If someone is playing soccer, baseball, basketball, or any other game in which a ball rolls, your Collie might quickly give chase..perhaps endangering its life should the ball roll into a busy thoroughfare. Always supervise your dog when playing outside.

make up a few rules of your own. If you don't follow the book, you'll get into jams you can't get out of by yourself. If after a few hours of short training sessions your Collie is still not working as he should, get back to the book for a study session, because it's your fault, not the dog's! The procedures of dog training have been so well systemized that it must be your fault, since literally thousands of fine Collies have been trained by the book.

After your Collie is "letter perfect" under all conditions, then, if you wish, go on to advanced training and trick work.

Your Collie will love his obedience training, and you'll burst with pride at the finished product! Your Collie will enjoy life even more, and you'll enjoy your Collie more. And remember—you *owe good training to your Collie.*

SHOWING YOUR COLLIE

A show Collie is a comparatively rare thing. He is one out of several litters of puppies. He happens to be born with a degree of physical perfection that closely approximates the standard by which the breed is judged in the show ring. Such a dog should, on maturity, be able to win or approach his championship in good, fast company at the larger shows. Upon finishing his championship, he is apt to be as highly desirable as a breeding animal. As a proven stud, he will automatically command a high price for service.

Showing Collies is a lot of fun—yes, but it is a highly competitive sport. While all the experts were once beginners, the odds are against a novice. You will be showing against experienced handlers, often people who have devoted a lifetime to breeding, picking the right ones, and then showing those dogs through to their championships. Moreover, the most perfect Collie ever born has faults, and in your hands the faults will be far more evident than with the experienced handler who knows how to minimize his Collie's faults. These are but a few points on the sad side of the picture.

The experienced handler, as I say, was not born knowing the ropes. He learned—*and so can you!* You can if you will put in the same time, study and keen observation that he did. But it will take time!

You should never take your Collie outside unless it is on a leash. The retractable leashes allow you to vary the walking distance between you and your dog. Photograph courtesy of Hagen.

KEY TO SUCCESS

First, search for a truly fine show prospect. Take the puppy home, raise him by the book, and as carefully as you know how, give him every chance to mature into

Scenes from dog shows with three color varieties of Collies.

the Collie you hoped for. My advice is to keep your dog out of big shows, even Puppy Classes, until he is mature. Maturity in the male is roughly two years; with the female, 14 months or so. When your Collie is approaching maturity, start out at match shows, and, with this experience for both of you, then go gunning for the big wins at the big shows.

Next step, read the standard by which the Collie is judged. Study it until you know it by heart. Having done this, and while your puppy is at home (where he should be) growing into a normal, healthy Collie, go to every dog show you can possibly reach. Sit at the ringside and watch Collie judging. Keep your ears and eyes open. Do your own judging, holding each of those dogs against the standard, which you now know by heart.

In your evaluations, don't start looking for faults. Look for the virtues—the best qualities. How does a given Collie shape up against the standard? Having looked for

and noted the virtues, then note the faults and see what prevents a given Collie from standing correctly or moving well. Weigh these faults against the virtues, since, ideally, every feature of the dog should contribute to the harmonious whole dog.

The exhibitor is holding a liver snack in her hand to get the Collie's attention during an outdoor dog show.

"RINGSIDE JUDGING"

It's a good practice to make notes on each Collie, always holding the dog against the standard. In "ringside judging," forget your personal preference for this or that feature. What does the standard say about it? Watch carefully as the judge places the dogs in a given class. It is difficult from the ringside always to see why number one was placed over the second dog. Try to follow the judge's reasoning. Later try to talk with the judge after he is finished. Ask him questions as to why he placed certain Collies and not others. Listen while the judge explains his placings, and, I'll say right

Winning Best of Breed makes the value of these Collies greatly enhanced for breeding purposes. Beside the fun and thrill of showing your Collie, you can collect ribbons, trophies and even financial rewards.

here, any judge worthy of his license should be able to give reasons.

When you're not at the ringside, talk with the fanciers and breeders who have Collies. Don't be afraid to ask opinions or say that you don't know. You have a lot of listening to do, and it will help you a great deal and speed up your personal progress if you are a good listener.

THE NATIONAL CLUB

You will find it worthwhile to join the national Collie club and to subscribe to its magazine. From the national club, you will learn the location of an approved regional club near you. Now, when your young Collie is eight to ten months old, find out the dates of match shows in your section of the country. These differ from regular shows only in that no championship points are given. These shows are especially designed to launch young dogs (and new handlers) on a show career.

This type of Collie can be called *white*, even though it has other markings. Check with your local dog club about entering a local dog show so you can get some experience in showing your Collie.

ENTER MATCH SHOWS

With the ring deportment you have watched at big shows firmly in mind and practice, enter your Collie in as many match shows as you can. When in the ring, you have two jobs. One is to see to it that your Collie is always being seen to its best advantage. The other job is to keep your eye on the judge to see what he may want you to do next. Watch only the judge and your Collie. Be quick and be alert; do exactly as the judge directs. Don't speak to him except to answer his questions. If he does something you don't like, don't say so. And don't irritate the judge (and everybody else) by constantly talking and fussing with your dog.

In moving about the ring, remember to keep clear of dogs beside you or in front of you. It is my advice to you *not* to show your Collie in a regular point show until he is at least close to maturity and after both you and your dog have had time to perfect ring manners and poise in the match shows.

GROOMING YOUR COLLIE

Unlike many breeds, Collies do not need a great deal of trimming, therefore, the grooming tools needed are neither numerous nor complicated. The ones you will need to do the job thoroughly—and by that I mean to groom a Collie for the show ring— are: radial nylon brush, wide-toothed comb (preferably steel), fine-toothed comb, straight sharp scissors, curved scissors, spray bottle, warm water, soap, sponge, towel, nail clippers, and large quantity of precipitated chalk. If you cannot get precipitated chalk, French chalk will do, or even corn flour.

There are two schools of thought on the subject of Collie grooming. Some owners belong to the "don't groom" school, others to the "groom daily." I advise you, if your Collie is a house pet, to place yourself somewhere between these two extremes. In my opinion more harm than good is done by grooming a Collie daily; but to leave him totally ungroomed is to ask for equal trouble because his coat will mat. Then, when you want to get him into good condition, it will be extremely difficult.

Shampoos especially good for Collies, both the dogs with rough and smooth coats, are available from your local pet shop or dog groomer. This shampoo cleans and conditions the Collie's coat making it shiny and soft. Photograph courtesy of Hagen.

Brushing your Collie really hard once a week is about all the grooming he should really need. He should never, and I repeat *never,* be bathed routinely. The only time a Collie should be bathed is when he's gotten into something he shouldn't have and there's no other way to clean him. If you want his white parts to look sparkling clean, wash them with a little warm water and detergent. But, to bathe a Collie all over is to destroy completely the natural oils in his coat, and it will take many weeks before they all build up again. Mud usually presents no problem because most of it dries up and falls out of the coat and a final brushing will get rid of what little remains. If you want your dog to look especially clean on some occasion, chalk through his white parts, then brush the chalk well out.

COMBING

The hair behind a Collie's ears is particularly soft and silky, and this is the hair most likely to mat; so check this area often. This, I think, is the only part of the coat that should be combed. To comb the coat all over is only to break and destroy it, but you will need a fine comb to remove the mats from behind the ears. If such mats form, they can interfere with the correct ear carriage. Very often the erect ear of a Collie is traceable to the fact that there are mats and hairballs behind it; so pay great attention to this point, even if your dog is only a house pet, not a show ring prospect.

SHEDDING

There is, however, one exception to the "no comb" rule.

When your dog begins to blow his coat in real earnest for the seasonal shedding, put your comb to work. Comb it at least daily, twice daily if you have the time, until the day arrives when no more hair will come out, and the Collie looks nearly naked. For the sooner you get rid of the dead hair, the faster the new coat will come in, and you will, once more be able to take pride in your lovely Collie.

Groomers use special grooming stands which keep the Collie at the proper height to make grooming easier for both the groomer and the dog.

EAR CARE

Daily ear examination is always wise. Never wash out a dog's ears with soap and water—not even the outer ear. If water gets deep into the ear, it is almost impossible to get it out, and it can present all kinds of problems. The best way to clean ears is with a cotton swab dipped into peroxide, alcohol or olive oil. Never probe deeper into the ear than you can see. If the ears seem unusually sensitive, or have a foul smell, it is wise to consult your vet. There are several good medicated dog ear washes on the market. Ask your favorite pet shop owner to recommend one.

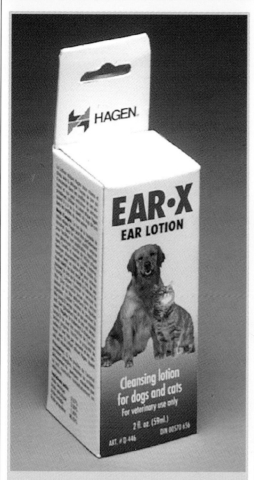

Keeping your Collie's ears clean is simple if you use a top quality lotion. It is essential that you maintain your Collie's ears, claws, teeth and fur. Photograph courtesy of Hagen.

Ear mange (Otodectic) sometimes called canker, is caused by rather large mites which infect the ear canal, causing painful irritation. The dog repeatedly shakes his head and scratches, crying and whining meanwhile. Soak a layer of cotton in mineral oil, wrap it around your index finger, and clean the ear with this gently.

There are many excellent cures for ear canker but scrupulous cleanliness helps most of all. The dark red discharge has a heavy unpleasant smell which will warn you of the mite's presence if the dog's misery and scratching at the base of the ear has not already pointed it out. Quite often a dog has been deemed "crabby" or shy when all that ailed him was ear mange.

EYE CARE

The eyes frequently collect foreign matter like seeds and pollen when the dog roams through high grass or ground cover. These can be irritating and, after such a venture, the eyes should be washed out with a commercial dog eye wash, or if none is at hand, luke-warm water.

Eyes that are constantly mattered-up and watering are suspect, and a veterinarian should be consulted. It may be the result of entropion—a hereditary condition in which the eyelids turn inward, or ectropion, when they turn outward. However, simple conjunctivitis—inflamed and watering eyes—can usually be dealt with at home. There are several reliable preparations on the market to combat it. Sometimes the gentle rubbing of sterile codliver oil on the upper and lower eyelid helps.

Any mucus in the eye-corners can be removed with a cotton-tipped swab dipped in lukewarm water.

SHOW RING GROOMING

Grooming for the show ring is a different matter. Again it is not necessary to groom him every day, even if he is a show dog, and certainly not to comb him; but when you decide to take your dog to a show, begin some weeks in advance to prepare him for the great day. This preparation need only consist of a regular twice weekly grooming, and at this stage, I would suggest, also that you begin to do any necessary trimming, because if you mistakingly overgroom him two

and where you show, which legs you trim. In Britain, only the hind legs are trimmed; in America, both the front and the hind legs come in for a certain amount of trimming.

Let us start with the hind legs, since their trimming is common to both countries. They need more trimming too. From the hocks, downwards, the hind legs will

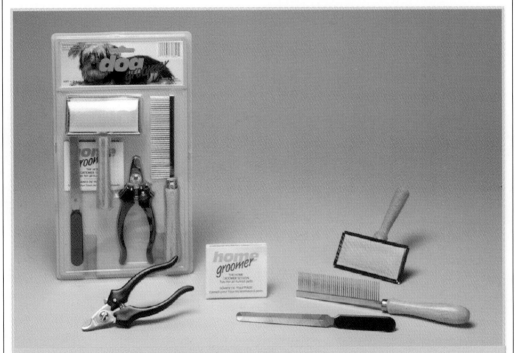

Unless you expect to have a professional groomer keep your Collie in proper condition, you should buy a grooming set. This is probably the most economical way to acquire the grooming tools you need. Grooming kits are available from your local pet shop. Photograph courtesy of Hagen.

weeks before the show, you will at least have a chance for nature to correct your errors. It is for this reason that I start with a discussion of trimming rather than grooming.

The legs are the only parts of the Collie that need careful trimming, and it depends on where you live

probably carry a great deal of long hair which must be trimmed off. Use a pair of straight scissors, trimming from the hock downwards. First of all, brush or comb the hair out, so that it stands at right angles to the leg, and then holding your scissors point down and parallel to the skin, cut in a downward direction. You will probably find it advisable to take the hair off in three or four scissorings rather than doing it all at once. It is almost as if you were mowing a lawn, except that you always go back to the same end to start.

The art is to round the hair off at the sides without leaving a sort of ditch in the middle with longer hair standing up on each side. Shorten the side hairs until they blend in with the hairs on the front of the legs.

In America, the custom is to cut some hair off the front of the legs as well.

Examine your dog's front legs until you find the black pad, which is just about under the knee. From this pad downwards the long hair should be treated exactly the same as the hair on the back legs—tidied off and feathered in well with the short hairs on the front.

Your next job is to tidy up your dog's feet. Take small scissors, preferably curved, and cut the hair between the pads away under each foot. Do not cut between the toes. Now trim right around the

If you want your Collie's coat to glisten, try an enhancer. This is a concentrate and one small bottle goes a long way. Photograph courtesy of Hagen.

outside of the paw until the hair is short, outlining the foot correctly. Then trim the hair round the toenails. This is probably easier to do with straight scissors. Have the dog stand on the foot you are trimming, preferably on a perfectly flat, hard surface like concrete. Watch that you have not left any odd strands of hair, and if so, clip them off before starting on the next foot. When you have done this successfully four times, you will be well on your way.

Some owners trim off the long whiskers on the dog's head, on either side of the muzzle and off the cheeks and eyebrows. This is something I never do. I consider it cruel. The fact that one can rarely cut these without an assistant to hold the dog proves that a dog's whiskers are just as sensitive as those of a cat, and no one would ever think of cutting them off a cat. However, as it is customary in some countries to trim these whiskers before the dog is shown, I can only add that if it must be done do it with curved scissors. To be safe, hold your

A professional dog groomer grooming a Collie. The dog should look extremely attractive after being groomed. It is up to you to keep your Collie looking like this for weeks after each grooming.

fingers over his eyes so that if he moves suddenly you won't stab them. Wisker trimming should be done only at the last moment—the night before the show at the earliest—because wiskers grow back quite rapidly, and you would not want your Collie to appear in the ring with a "five o'clock shadow."

Returning now to the trimming that can be started a couple of weeks before the show, look at your dog's ears and see whether around them, either in front or back, there are long straggly strands of hair. If so, they should be carefully removed. Do this with the thumb and finger, twisting them out a few at a time. It causes only a twinge of pain—like plucking eyebrows and if you have two weeks to complete the job, a few hairs can be stripped out each day without creating a hardship for either of you. Do not remove too many hairs, as that would tend to give him a hard expression. Where the hairs are long and straggly, or curling inside the ear, they should certainly be removed.

Having performed this initial trimming, keep an eye on the ears so that, if the hairs grow back before the show, you have time to pluck them. The speed at which each hair grows, particularly on the hind legs, varies tremendously from dog to dog. Some Collies rarely need this part of the leg trimmed at all. Others look like Clydesdale horses, and seem to grow their feathering in a matter of days.

Now take a brush. For this job I prefer a radial nylon brush. It gets down to the skin of the dog, and the spaces between the bristles allow greater penetration. With this brush go over the dog from head to foot, starting at the head end and working down, making absolutely certain that no mats are left anywhere. If you do find a mat, get to work with your wide-toothed comb until each hair is seperated again. After this initial preperation, done some two weeks before the show, go over him at least every second day with your nylon brush, just to make sure that no fresh mats are forming, taking special pains behind the ears. Be sure that the soft hair there does not bunch up and become unsightly.

This brings us to the day before the show. Now, you will again do everything I have suggested, and one or two other things as well. Check your dogs toenails, making sure they are not too long. This, in fact, in Collies is rare, but if you think that the white of the toenail is too far extended from the quick (which can be seen showing pink within the white) snip the tip of the nail. Tidy up the feet again if necessary.

Next, you will want a bucket of warm water with a detergent. Put the dog's legs one by one in this bucket, washing them thoroughly until they are sparkling clean. Also, wash his white shirt front, and his collar and tail tip if it is white. Rub the dog until he is nearly dry, then chalk these white parts. Brush the chalk well into the foot, the leg, the collar and the tail tip. Leave the chalk in the fur at least overnight. If you think there is a chance of his getting dirty on the way to the show, or at the entrance to the show, leave the chalk in until after your arrival, because, when you brush it out, any dirt aquired on the journey will come with it. However, by the time you get to the show there probably won't be a great deal of chalk left, because the dog will have shaken it out during the night.

Remember to arrive at the show in plenty of time. You will probably need at least an hour to get yourself and your dog in readiness. The white parts must almost certainly be rechalked on arrival, and it is often wise to wash and chalk the legs once more. You cannot, of course, wash shirt front and collar again at this late stage because they would take too long to dry. After rechalking your dog, go over him

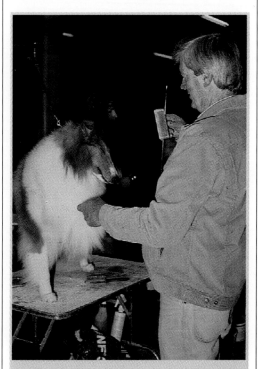

This Collie is being brushed with a special dog brush. Pet shops carry many different kinds of dog brushes, though it might be more economical to buy a complete grooming set.

again with your nylon brush, until each hair is standing out seperately. You can also run your comb through the hair as well, if you think that this will help. Remember, though, that you must never take your dog into the show ring with chalk still on him. Brush out every particle before going into the ring. If the judge detects chalk on the dog's coat, he

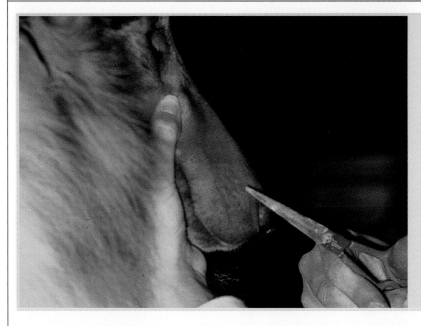

Whisker cutting should be done only on show Collies, and only the night before the show since the whiskers grow back so quickly.

may well disqualify him. So be careful.

Now for one of the final touches: Take a spray—an ordinary spray bottle—filled with either fresh water, or 50% water and 50% of one of the many advertised coat dressings, and parting the hair at appropriate places spray it against his skin. Your object is to make the undercoat really damp, but not the long hairs on top. A damp undercoat will help to keep the top coat standing off, giving the impression that your dog has a larger coat than he really has. This spraying should be done straight along his back and on his sides, and on his flanks. Then start to brush, and brush, and brush, and brush, and brush. The object is to get him nearly dry, but not quite dry, and leave the top coat stansding off.

This last brush should be done just before he goes into the ring. Then, as a last minute touch, make certain that his mane is beautifully brushed out, that the hair under his tail is equally well-treated, and that the feathers on his front legs stand out as they should. Then take your nylon brush and, very gently, flatten the long top coat the full length of his backbone from head to tail root and just a little over his sides as well, because you do not want him to go into the ring looking like a large wooly bear. His coat must appear to fit him, but it must also appear to be beautiful and heavy.

If your dog is to be shown at a number of shows within a short period, all that you will need do, having got him ready for his first show, is to check regularly that he is not becoming matted behind the ears, that his feet remain tidy, and that the feathering on his back legs does not need cutting. Other than this, the pre-show day damping and chalking and regular brushing are all that should be necessary after your arrival at the show.

YOUR HEALTHY COLLIE

Your Collie is the image of good health: a glistening, clean coat, clear eyes, pink gums, moist nose, and ever-alert and active. We know our pets, their moods and habits, and therefore we can recognize when our Collie is experiencing an off-day. Signs of sickness can be very obvious or very subtle. As any mother can attest, diagnosing and treating an ailment requires common sense, knowing when to seek home remedies and when to visit your doctor, or veterinarian, as the case may be.

Your veterinarian, we know, is your Collie's best friend, next to you. It will pay to be choosy about your veterinarian. Talk to dog owning friends whom you respect. Visit more than one vet before you make a lifelong choice. Trust your instincts. Find a knowledgeable, compassionate vet who knows Collies and likes them.

Keep this first aid cream on hand in cases of cuts as it is antiseptic and sterilizes wounds. Photograph courtesy of Hagen.

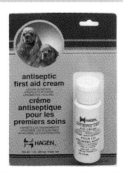

VACCINATIONS

For the continued health of your dog, owners must attend to vaccinations regularly. Your veterinarian can recommend a vaccination schedule appropriate for your dog taking into consideration the factors of climate and geography. The basic vaccinations to protect your dog are: parvovirus, distemper, hepatitis, leptospirosis, adenovirus, parainfluenza, coronavirus, bordetella, tracheobronchitis (kennel cough), Lyme disease and rabies.

Parvovirus is a highly contagious, dog-specific disease, first recognized in 1978. Targeting the small intestine, parvo affects the stomach and diarrhea and vomiting (with blood) are clinical signs. Although the dog can pass the infection to other dogs within three days of infection, the initial signs, which include lethargy and depression, don't display themselves until four to seven days. When affecting puppies under four weeks of age, the heart muscle is frequently attacked. When the heart is affected, the puppies exhibit difficulty in breathing and experience crying and foaming at the nose and mouth.

Distemper, related to human measles, is an airborne virus that spreads in the blood and ultimately in the nervous system and epithelial tissues. Young dogs or dogs with weak immune systems can develop encephalomyelitis (brain disease) from the distemper infection. Such dogs experience seizures, general weakness and rigidity, as well as "hardpad." Since distemper is largely incurable, prevention through vaccination is vitally important. Puppies should be vaccinated at six to eight weeks of age, with boosters at ten to 12 weeks. Older puppies (16 weeks and older) who are unvaccinated should receive no fewer than two vaccinations at three to four week intervals.

Bordetella, called canine cough, causes a persistent hacking cough in dogs and is very contagious.

Rabies is passed to dogs and people through wildlife: in North America, principally through the skunk, fox and raccoon; the bat is not the culprit it was once thought to be. Likewise, the common image of the rabid dog foaming at the mouth with every hair on end is unlikely the truest scenario. A rabid dog exhibits difficulty eating, salivates much and has spells of paralysis and awkwardness. Before a dog reaches this final state, it may experience anxiety, personality changes, irritability and more aggressiveness than is usual. Vaccinations are strongly recommended as affected dogs are too dangerous to manage and are commonly euthanized. Puppies are generally vaccinated at 12 weeks of age, and then annually.

HEARTWORM IN COLLIES

Heartworm disease is transmitted by mosquitoes and badly affects the lungs, heart and blood vessels of dogs. The larvae of Dirofilaria immitis enter the dog's bloodstream when bitten by an infected mosquito. The larvae take about six months to mature. Infected dogs suffer from weight loss, appetite loss, chronic coughing and general fatigue. Not all affected dogs show signs of illness right away, and carrier dogs may be affected for years before clinical signs appear. Treatment of heartworm disease is generally effective for most other breeds, but can be very dangerous for Collies especially. Prevention as always is the desirable alternative. Ivermectin, the active ingredient in most heartworm preventatives, has caused unfavorable reaction in Collies and should likely be avoided. Discuss your options with your veterinarian and be sure he is familiar with the latest developments in the Collies and Ivermectin debate.

The best book on a dog's health is the one written by Dr. Lowell Ackerman and called OWNER'S GUIDE TO DOG HEALTH. Written in simple, easy-to-understand language, it is the most comprehensive single volume of its kind.